THE
Phases
OF THE
Soul

CARLOS MEDINA

Thank you to all the people that have supported me through this journey. Many thanks to Leda Zaidi and Naticha Hernandez for helping me in the editorial process. I'm grateful for all the lessons I have learned throughout my life. I wouldn't be here if it weren't for them. A special thanks to my parents, for encouraging me to keep going and never looking back. I'm truly grateful for the unknown. It sent a mesmerizing rare soul to cross my path and awakened this deep love I have. To all my followers on Instagram and Facebook. This one is for you.

Carlos Medina

Let me intoxicate you with passion,
Let me take your breath away.
Surrender me your heart and I will promise to give you
my all.
Let me fix what's broken and
I'll open up the door for you.

Her eyes were like splashes of holy water, burning deep in my soul.

I customized every piece of my heart, in preparation for the journey my soul was going to take.

In life, you kill your old self many times just so you can find that right person. You search and search for this person that you dream of daily. You meet many people and one by one you begin to nitpick them. You begin to see all their failures or things that don't agree with you. Suddenly your desire to find the right one fades away. Then one day out of nowhere, someone crosses your path. They show you things about yourself that you never saw. You begin to feel weird emotions within. Your heart races faster than normal. Your mind begins to go in full effect and bypasses all those feelings. Throughout the day, you still have the thought of that person. It's a pure and heartfelt feeling. It's a beautiful thing you feel. You feel that for once in your life, someone truly understands you for you. When someone crosses your path and you feel this way. Let it all out. Showcase your vulnerability to them. Above all, showcase your soul to them. It's the most beautiful thing a person could ever do.

Close your eyes and shut down your mind.. feel my words touching your heart, allow my soul to construct the universe in which you want to call home.

Her love never had a price. It just demanded pure love, honesty and integrity.

As beautiful souls that we are, we need to know when to take control of our feelings and emotions. We often give a lot more than we should and I understand why we do this. For we have so much love bottled inside that we want to give it out. We fall for others quickly for we see that we can be their missing link. Then as time passes we see that it's not going the way we wanted and I know deep inside you feel that this person is the one. You share so much with them and you begin to be so vulnerable with them that you truly desire to be by their presence. At night you imagine all the possibilities of you both together that you can actually feel their spirit next to you. Just keep in mind that this is a two way street and if they don't show you the same love, interest or affection.. then it's time to pause for a minute and realize that you will get hurt. Two souls in true love will break boundaries. Love is felt within it's powerful and it's pure. It's not a game.

Surrendering my mind was the hardest thing to do but it was the only way to allow my soul to take full control.

I closed my eyes and touched her soul. Words will never describe the feeling, for it's something not meant for the mind to understand.. but when you close your eyes and speak to another person. You have managed to speak the language of a higher power unknown to mankind.

As time went by, I realized that my soul had become extremely powerful. I've tried to hold back so many things that I found within but the reality is.. my love is a carbon copy of you.

Not many people you come across in life will have the same intentions as you. Some will come and try to hurt you, some will come and tease you, and few will come and love you. Those that try to hurt you are the ones that have been hurt many times before.. and to be honest, they don't know any better than hurting others. Those that come around to tease you are just doing it for pleasure. Keep in mind that those are just passing by to stimulate their egos. Be careful with your emotions and feelings, you will get attached and hurt.. I assure you that. Those that come and love you.. appreciate and understand that they really know what pain is. They have been hurt, teased and loved. They have suffered more than you can imagine. They have this tremendous amount of love bottled inside, that if they opened up to you, you will feel all of their love pouring out. Understand that the only way they know how to show you their feelings and emotions is by trusting you. Once you've obtained that. You have basically opened the gates to their souls. Yes. Those are the rare ones that live amongst us. We see them everyday. They are the ones that have that depth in their eyes. That with a single stare you begin to see their lives in front of you. Perhaps those are what they call the old souls or broken souls. But to me, those are the soulmates crawling this earth in search for their other.

We live by faith. We have this faith that one day we will find that soulmate. That somewhere, throughout the world there is that one person meant for us. We seek daily for this love that's unconditional. We seek for this pure love. We desire this soul next to us. A person that will see our imperfections and know that it's just us and they will understand us. They are capable of freezing their time just to spend it with us. These souls have a special gift. They will make you see yourself through their eyes. You will begin to finally feel wanted and cherished. Your heart will skip many beats, for what you feel cannot be explained. They have this strength to turn your dreams and fantasies into reality. Understanding you comes as second nature to them. For what you see in them is your future being unfold.

It's my need to come find you.
I'm getting addicted to your mind.
Within me you will find where your soul belongs.
Leave your feelings behind and lay your heart to rest.

When they finally meet and stare at each other. Their souls will ignite. That's when the collision of two soul-mates begin.

Most of the times, we broken souls make a common mistake. We fall in love quickly. We fall for others in a blink of an eye. Why? For we have been through so much in life that we are dying to fall in love.. but we forget that we should fall in love with their souls first. We make the mistake of catching these crazy feelings for others. Since we have been through so much, we don't want to see them hurt. We create an illusion that those people need us in their lives and the reality is, my friend, that we can't help them. We can't force anyone to feel the way we feel, even if your intuition tells you they are the one. If you don't receive the same passion you are giving, well.. I'm sorry but it's time to move on. Yes, I know it will hurt and it will sting you hard. But trust me, it's better to walk away and feel a little hurt than keep pushing for something that you will never get or even share with them. Today is the day that you must take a step back and look at what you have done. Look at all the effort you have put into it. Look at it and ask yourself will this work? Of course, you will want to say yes.. but let's be realistic here. Does it seem like it will go further? Does the other person share this same vision as you? If not, then it's time to reanalyze your position here. Love is a two way street my friends. Not a one way street.

It's hard, I know.

The times, memories, special moments..

Just remember you did all you could and now is time to move on.

And at night while lying down in the darkest hours. The time when you feel my presence through your thoughts, and your imagination runs wild. Understand, that I can feel it too. It's not the desires of our souls, but the fear of not predicting the outcome is what keeps our hearts far apart.

I didn't look at you as a temporary spot holder. When I saw you, I truly believed in something magical. Perhaps it's your hidden love that attracted my soul to find you.. but as time passed by I finally understood that the reality is, you just showed me the greatest lesson a man can learn. It's the power of unleashing my soul to the whole world.

Daily, I saw you in my dreams. I envisioned your soul close to me. I hungered constantly for a taste of your love. Come take my hand, allow me to welcome you to my reality.

She craved. She wanted to know all the secrets hidden in this addicted mind. She desired the passion held within. She sought attention, affection and love. Once she looked into my eyes, she knew that my soul was her home.

She just wanted to be loved. The way she loved.

In life we offer our love to many people that we feel some-
thing special about. We feel this beautiful thing within
ourselves about them. For once we feel alive. The way
they make us feel, we completely surrender everything
for them. We go and dig deep within ourselves just to
give them a glimpse of the beautiful and precious love we
have to offer. Why? Why do we do this? For we know that
they deserve every single drop of love we have left. We go
and court them, we treat them differently from so many
other people. We honor them. We respect them. We cher-
ish them. We allow our soul to just go and caress their soul
and touch their hearts in many ways. We don't just stim-
ulate their minds, we captivate their spirit. We welcome
their presence into our lives. What is the result? Some will
become soulmates for their souls acknowledge each other.
While some will never understand what we have to offer.
They allow their minds to take over everything. They sink
in and become prisoners to their thoughts. It's unfortu-
nate that they will never know what could've been when
two powerful souls unite.. but guess what? They will see
you when you move on and you will find someone else. I
promise you that you will, and that thought will forever
linger in the back of their minds.. what if? Remember
there is a limit to what you can do in courting another
soul. Not all souls are meant to be your soulmate. Rare
are those. If you did it all, and you don't even get a sign or
a let's take it slow and get to know each other: Just thank
them and walk away. Don't hurt your soul in the courting
stage. You already did all you could do. Now it's time to
go and allow your soul to drift into the unknown.

Those that are singles in this world go through a lot of internal pain. It's true. Not many will know this. For they hide it very well from the world. It's the pain of going to bed alone and waking up alone. Not sharing your life with someone. Not feeling the love desired by someone. Just being completely alone. It hurts. Not holding someone's hand while walking down the street or shopping. Not having someone to share dinner with. This list could go on and on. As time passes, your love just fades away. You stop believing in that powerful force. You begin to think, no one will love me the way I always wanted to be loved. Do you know that you're not alone in those thoughts? Many people think and feel the same way. They are just like you and me. Thinking the same thing and saying the exact same thing. That love that you believed from a young age.. it will come to you. Trust me. When you allow your soul to guide you, it will attract what it's seeking. I have always believed it. As time went by, I lost myself in the thoughts of love: it is generated by two individuals' needs. But what happens when the need of one is not a need no more? They leave! They leave and to try and smooth shit out they say, I have to go find myself. I believe love is a strong powerful feeling from two individuals. It's the craving of the others soul. It's your spirit yearning for theirs. It's being able to see a future with the other person. If you can't see that... Don't go for it. It's a mutual commitment. A respect from both. An understanding of their imperfections, and still feeling the same towards them. It's a desire from within for the other person. It's a sacrifice. It's being touched and understood in many ways. It's finishing each other's sentences. It's not a mental thing. It's a soulful thing. It has to be pure. It has to be honest. It has to be loyal.

When my soul manifests itself on to you, Allow it. Feel it. Cherish it. Above all, adore it. For what it says are things that no one has ever heard and are customized just for you.

She was not interested in looking for a sexual encounter. She was looking for something with more meaning. She didn't care how you looked. She cared how you felt within. She didn't want her soul touched with dirty hands. She wanted someone real. With internal powers. With a magic that can penetrate deep in her soul. Forget mind stimulating. She wanted her spirit stimulated from your soul.

She loves poetry. She fantasies daily about her future love. She feels his vibes daily in the air she breathes, and they are becoming addicting. She knows for a fact that the time is approaching when their eyes will meet. She is aware of his luring eyes and the way his passion erupts from his soul, but that's not her worry at all. Her worry is mostly can he live up to his words and not turn out like the rest.

Tell me all about your pain. Tell me all your secrets. Let me sit here and absorb them all. I promise you I won't let you go through them alone. Together side by side we will collide until the end of time.

And in the midst of her pain, she searched for guidance. She felt that the whole world was against her. She wanted someone to hold her in their arms, to kiss her forehead and to show her that everything will be alright. All she ever wanted was for that special guy to come and prove to her that dreams do come true. That one guy that will rip all of her pain from her heart. That one guy that will listen, understand and cherish her for who she really is. Just for once she wanted that one person with so much understanding and power to elevate her soul to another dimension where love never dies. Where their unity will become a powerful force.

Sometimes as human beings we take for granted what we have. Some people actually do find that person that they have been searching for their entire life. Seriously they do, but why they never end up with them? For so much goes on in their minds that they either hesitate or just don't believe that this is actually happening to them. They allow the doubts to sink in and they question every single thing that is occurring to them at that moment with the other person. They fear. They fear that whatever happened in their past, has a good chance to happen again. So they wait. They wait to see if it's true, the emotions they feel. While waiting, they go and explore. For now, they are not looking through their third eye. They are looking at the outer appearance and everything that catches the human eye. Instead, let's look at what catches the attention of our souls.

She has that pure beauty within her. The one that makes you believe, when you don't understand.

A day with you would be like a year. God, wouldn't I give to spend ten years with you. That's priceless.

Sometimes walking away is not giving up. It's knowing that you will no longer be part of the game that others play. When you feel that you have given your all into something and don't see something in return.. walk away. You will end up getting hurt. Perhaps not physically, but emotionally. If they really wanted to be a part of your life they would make an effort to be. It's not about all the times that you give. You need to feel some love too. If you absolutely know that you have left everything on the table and they have held back or hesitated. Keep it moving. They are not meant for you or they are just simply stuck in their past. It's understandable what you felt. You are not alone. Your feelings matter here, above all.. you matter. I will never say it will be easy. It's not.. but let's be honest.. how much more can you keep going at it? You could, but you'll end up hurt. If you're the one always seeking them and checking up on them and they never even say have a good day.. That's a sign right there. Someone that appreciates you and loves you will always check up on you. A simple good morning or goodnight text, or have a nice day. Something so simple, and yet so many fail at it.

I created an orchestra of many syllables in search for your soul.

I pinned her against the wall. Pressed my lips on her neck. Whispering all those magical words to her ear. She opened her eyes and showed me the coalition of two souls in love.

When the fog clears, you will see the light.. and finally you will understand why you had to walk in the dark for so long.

And finally, my spirit was free. Gliding through the night I finally saw her. Laying in bed soaking her pillow. I touched her soul in order to feel her emotions. She had this string of hair covering her face, gently I placed it behind her ear. So many silent tears running down her cheek, I couldn't resist but to kiss them away. Feeling my heartbeats close to hers she knew that nothing on earth could stop this powerful force.

As I close my eyes, I tune myself into you. I become you. The feelings become vivid. Your memories are fresh on my mind. Your past pain is cutting my heart with its straight razor, but the love you still have is pouring like rain into my soul.

When I love.. I love the flaws, imperfections, scars, shattered heart, crazy thoughts, and broken soul. When I love, I just adore you in whole. For I know underneath all of the layers is a gold mine hidden in your soul.

Have patience and wait. Wait for me. Hold those tears in for just a little longer. I promise you I will kiss them away. Just understand that this part of the journey must be done alone and if you decide that you cannot handle the pressure of time. Do not worry. I will understand. Forever I shall cherish the times our souls interacted with each other. And until death, I will remember the times our hearts synced as one.

Some people will come into our lives and make a tremendous impact. It will be felt in your core and you will easily fall for their soul. They will treat you in such a beautiful way that slowly you will become addicted to them. You will see all their imperfections as perfections and you will feel so wonderful around them, that your heart just fucking melts. You will tell yourself "shit!, this person is the one". This person sees me for me. What happens then? You begin to think about this person daily and every freakin' hour that passes by, you imagine your life with this person. So, you begin to elevate your conversations to a higher Level. REMEMBER YOU, not them. Step back and see things differently. You allow your soul to scream out all of its silent cries to them. You tell them so many deep secrets and become so vulnerable to them, and you give them so many hints about how you feel. What happens next? They agree to what you say and leave your thoughts in the air. Guess what? Now you're confused and you don't know what are their intentions. If something like this has or is happening in your life. Don't get discouraged that they never told you how they feel towards you. Remember, not all people can love the way you do and not everyone you think could be your soulmate is actually your soulmate. Some people are just passing by. They are just those individuals that are here to show you that you still have love within. That is all. If someone makes you confused or makes you doubt if they have the same feelings towards you, perhaps they are one of those souls passing by. Don't hate them or hold anything against them. As a matter a fact, thank them.. thank them for showing you that love still exist within you and it's ok, you will cry for a while, for those feelings were deep. Learn that if a person truly has some feelings towards you beyond friendship, they will tell you. Especially after you tell them. Your love is deep and it's not meant for all. The right one will see it and tell you that they can see a future with you and the elevation of both will begin.

And after all the hurt. I still managed to rise and show how much love I have within.

I didn't give up on you. I just walked away from the bull-shit you let out that was hidden within you.

She loved reading poetry. It was her escape from reality. When she read it, she became it in her imagination. She searched through all of them for signs. Signs about her current situation and about what her future would bring. She believed in something beyond the understanding of any human. Although all the signs were there, the burnt holes left in her heart from the past were still hurting the most.

Miles separated them. Point of views separated them. Beliefs separated them. The thoughts separated them. Hesitation separated them. When it's true love.. nothing will ever separate two souls.

One thing I learned from my past relationship was, how to truly love a person. I thought that by doing epic things for my ex was the best way to show my love.. but it's not. They don't want fancy things. After failures I learned that it really is the simple things that shows your true love. A random call/text just to say hi or I love you. Sometimes.. sometimes it only takes her to hear you say things from your heart. Trust me. She can feel it when it's from your heart and truly meant. Mean the words - you're beautiful, gorgeous, adorable, my love, hun, baby, etc. mean them. Appreciate her for all she has done. If sometimes you think she hasn't done anything. Guess what? Appreciate her for being by your side. For sticking by you in good and bad. Demonstrate your passion for her. Don't let her do everything around the house. Take a Saturday and go help her do the laundry. Make her a sandwich for lunch. For fucks sakes, if you don't know how to cook, Google that shit or YouTube it. The tools are there. Use them. Ask her what's her favorite food. Give her a bubble bath. If that sounds weird, jump in with her in the tub and give her a back massage. Pour some lavender scent in the water, pop open some champagne and just relax, the both of you. Forget the world for a moment. Put the soft music on. Make love. Touch her body like the world was ending. Just you and her. No phones. Just two souls making love.

And if for once.. just once, could I hold you in my arms. It would be the way to allow you to feel the security you always wanted and if it would be the first and last time, just look into my eyes and see what I hold inside. If you don't feel what I feel, I promise to walk away and leave you with the most beautiful goodbye.

We search for the right one. We seek for that other person that fits into the small space in our hearts and we come across many that looks like a fit but are not. Rarely we find a few that fit perfectly in our hearts and it scares the shit out of us. We begin to wonder is this truly happening? We question everything about them. We question their acts, words, actions, way of living.. everything we question. Why? We are just shocked that something like this could happen to us. The worst part about it is, we question ourselves. Are we enough? What do we have that they like? How could they seriously like me? Or better yet.. who am I for this person to feel those feelings towards me? Sometimes it's better, an oops than a what if and while this whole process is happening we begin to say to ourselves, let me see if the universe sends me signs or someone else. What happens? We loose sight of what's in front of us while we look more into the unknown. Not realizing that sometimes what's in front of us is a fit to our heart or the missing link to our soul. My whole point to this is, cherish what you have at the moment. These souls are rare nowadays.. and when I say rare, I mean RARE.

Sometimes we ask ourselves why? Why did we have to go through all the pain we encountered in our past. Well, by going through all of it.. we learn. We learn to survive, to feel, to understand, to cherish, to self love. Above all.. WE LEARN TO LIVE.

It's not how much I could love. It's more of, how much depth can people handle. See, I had to learn something in my healing stage. I had to learn that loving someone has to be with depth. It's not all about the beautiful words and the way we craft them. It's how deep you can go within yourself and pull out those words. When you dive into your soul and bypass so many layers. You will find something within that's so beautiful and pure. You begin to really feel love in a different way. You will see things differently too. Somehow the empath level rises in you. As time goes by, I become more cautious. I could never ask a person to give me in return the same love I give. It's impossible.. but I will never settle for nothing less than purity, trust and love. Remember, intuition is the voice of the soul. Listen to it. Seems hard sometimes but it will guide you in the right path.

I'm breaking all traditions just to find your soul.

Remember in true love, there are no boundaries. There is no limit to the amount of love you can show your partner. It's not about the expensive things, like the diamond rings or the high end purses. It's mostly the small things that matter. Simple things as taking a nice walk. You don't have to wait for a special occasion to buy her a nice 'I love you' card or just tell her to relax for one day, and go take care of all the chores around the house. Maybe one day you should put that apron on and bake a nice cake for her. Small things, guys. They seem hard, but they are actually easy to do. Better yet, get the nail polish and paint her nails one day. Nothing wrong with a man showing his love towards his woman. If you really think that's going overboard.. go get the baby oil and give her a nice body massage. I bet you she will love that. Hey, you never know. She'll probably take good care of you later on in the evening.

She didn't need someone to help her through it. She just wanted someone to be there with her through it.

And although I'm gone, understand that I'm still here. I may not have been the one that you desired, but i know my soul spoke and touched you in many unknown forms. Perhaps it was just a lesson for our spirits to finally understand that there is a reality in the fantasies we play in our minds. Maybe we will never understand what we actually felt, but one thing I know for sure.. our souls and hearts will cherish and remember those magical times.

I did what most men feared the most. I allowed my soul to speak to you in the most vulnerable form unknown to all human being. Perhaps it was a mistake or the best thing you have ever felt but just knowing that I touched you in so many untouchable ways.. I can rest assured I did the right thing.

When two lost souls find each other the connection is unexplainable and intense. They begin to explore each other in many ways just to assure that it's not a mistake. They allow the other into the deepest parts of their souls for they feel that the other person understands everything about them. They open this beautiful communication between each other that many people wonder what the hell are they saying. Slowly they open their hearts. For some it's a quick opening, for others it's a longer process. It all depends on the past hurt. If the connection is mutual.. do not worry, time means nothing when both souls are being vulnerable to each other. Just make sure you know what are your intentions from the beginning and make them aware of it too. Never take advantage of a soul that has been hurt by its past. Remember karma is a bitch and has no mercy. When you court a soul like this, understand that they will come with a lot of hurt and suffering from the past. Just like you.. you'll have to have a great amount of patience and understanding and respect them. Respect them for they have survived and continue to strive from the previous hurt. Cherish them. Demonstrate that love you hold within. Finally, when you look into their eyes.. you must see a future with them. You have to be that person that will bring them out of the past. You must have that power within you. It's that sacred pure power of true love that will revive their love. Surrender the mind to your soul, and watch how powerful your spirit will become.

It happens like this. You lose hope in love. You forget to love yourself. You've been hurt so many times that you say, that's it. I will never fall in love. You stop looking around for that other beautiful soul, for you don't believe any longer. Then one day, one day someone comes and crosses your path. They tell you things that you can't believe. They see through your eyes everything and it scares you a bit. For never in your life someone saw you for you, and you begin to think about that person through out the day. When you're driving you imagine life with that person. You begin to study everything about them. For you feel deep within a connection that your soul desired so long. Then, slowly this person turns around all your feelings and emotions and you feel this love towards them that it seems so hard to explain. You fear saying it for you think that it's weird the way you feel. But, it's not.. it's not weird at all. Sometimes a person like that can make you feel something within that a person you loved and lived with didn't. It's called pure soul love. It's depth cannot be described but, it can be felt deeply. Someone that can understand you and be there for you at any given time. That's a keeper. It's hard to find souls like that nowadays, but if you are lucky and come across one.. Hold on to them. They may have that key to your heart.

Love her. Shower her with that love you have within. Be that soul that digs deep into her. Pamper her. Take her for a midnight drive. Cuddle with her. Watch her favorite shows. Massage her back and caress her body. When you touch her skin, feel her softness gliding through your fingers. Kiss her forehead to allow her to feel the security within you. Look into her eyes and tell her how much you adore her. Make sure she feels the intensity in you. When you lay her in bed, make sure your soul is making love to hers.

Never fall for that cheap love shit. Remember you deserve every inch of the love a person holds within their soul. That bullshit new love they call shouldn't even be acknowledged. You want depth. You want a person to love every single fucking part of your soul and nothing less. Never settle. Make sure you push their boundaries and see if it's pure love. You will feel it within when their pureness pours out.

I drained myself trying to touch below her skin. The layer that many never saw for she kept well secured. I isolated myself from this world just to reformat my inner self. I studied her inside out, but never did I try to manipulate her mind. While many play the game of words, I took them all and created my own alphabet, the one that no one has ever heard except for her soul. Maybe, just maybe my soul managed to make her feel something special.. something unique, an impact like no other. A chance to be held by a fallen angel. Then again, I could just be that ancient soul that passes by to revive the lost love.

Somebody will take your heart in. They will bring out that love in you. They'll bring you out of that shell you're in. Then for once in your life, you will understand that there is a person out there that can love you with so much heart and soul.

As your thoughts scribble pain through the chambers of your brain, just tap my heart and watch my soul take you away.

She broke into my imagination in ways that no one has. I gave her access to my soul knowing she can always claim it as hers.

If you love her, truly love her.. show her. Take that step out of the box and show her that pure love you hold. Make her understand that it was not a mistake to fall in love with you. Play with her sometimes. It's not all about being romantic. It's about sharing your life with this special person. It's about seeing your future with her. Surprise her. It's not always about the expensive things. It's the small things that counts. Those that come from your heart. Print a beautiful picture of you guys and frame it. Hang it on the wall before she comes in from work. I'll bet you she will love it. Go to a stationary store, buy transfer paper and iron a portrait of you guys on the shirt. Make sure you make two.. one for her and one for you. Have it on before she comes home. Lay down next to her and ask her how was her day. Listen to what she says and understand that she too has some rough ones. When she is washing the dishes, stand behind her and help her. I'm positively sure she will love that and so will you. Don't be ashamed of doing things around the house too. It's not only her job it's yours too. Go wash the laundry for her. What? You're embarrassed to fold her underwear? C'mon now, you're not embarrassed to take them off from her! What I'm trying to say is, just love her and show it from your heart. Plain and simple. Love the shit out of her. For she loves you enough to trust you with her heart and soul.

If I gave you my heart, would you dare to claim my soul?

Understand, that I'm here for you. I have heard your soul every night and its felt my presence deep within. I whispered into your ear those beautiful angelic words just so you can get a taste of this powerful unknown. They say time and distance could separate two individuals. They just forgot to mention that time and distance can create an internal fire between two powerful souls.

And if just for one night. Let's allow tonight to be that night where we give in to our thoughts. Let's stop playing hide and seek, and just close our eyes. Let's see within each other what our past failed to see. Come closer and lay here with me. Allow me to tattoo your body with sweet kisses. Don't worry, after tonight your soul will understand the true definition of the eternal love it deserved.

Let me make love to you while the night is young. Better yet.. let's wait until midnight so the wolf in me can come out and howl at your soul.

How do you know it's true love? When every chance you get during the day you catch yourself thinking about that person. Not in a sexual way, but a pure soulful way. When you begin to see a future with that person. When your heart desires so much to be in the same vicinity with them. When you wake up and the first thing that crosses your mind is that person. When you can't fall asleep because that person is on your mind. When you can actually trust that person with the most sacred possession, your heart. When that person uplifts and support you in good and bad. When that person acknowledges and cherishes you completely. The way you both can communicate and understand each other's point of view. The loyalty and commitment towards you and the relationship. The love they demonstrate towards you. Most important of all, the way you can feel their open soul.

When in a relationship, you need to showcase the love. There are many ways to do that. Be the weird ones. Take pictures together.. many pictures. Go take a walk in the city, hold hands - it's a sign of giving the other security. Take a ride in the middle of the night. Words don't have to be said, but spending those precious moments together speak volumes. Go to the movies, have a picnic, go hiking.. enjoy that fresh air and enjoy each other's souls. Remember, it's the commitment within each other that brings the soulmates.

We drowned in each other's depth as if there was no life-guard. We knew it was never touched by our past, so we felt unique knowing that we were the first.. and for sure the only ones to dive into it. For many it was a sacred place that existed only in the imagination but for us it was the place we made a reality of.

I came back from the grave just to find you. I heard your soul calling me in the middle of the night for a long time. I needed to destroy that old me, for it wasn't right for you. That old me was just an illusion.. now this is the real me. Constructed with unknown powers to guide and support you to the future. Just close your eyes, take my hand and allow me to elevate the love we have inside to a place where love never dies.

We fall in and out of love. It's part of life. For a period of time we feel happy in a relationship, and unhappy.. and what happens when we think we found that person that can take us with them to the future? They fuck up and show us their true colors as times goes on and we get hurt. Hurt emotionally, physically or mentally. We begin to blame ourselves. What did I do wrong? Why don't you love me anymore? Words that we say when we are the ones feeling all the pain and while we are drowning in our pain, they are partying and exploring others. Many of us have been through that road. I know I have been there but I'll tell you something, that pain you feel it will not hurt for long. I promise you it won't and when you think you could never find someone that could love you the way you always dreamed of, you're wrong. Trust me. There is someone out there with the same amount of love as you. They are asking the unknown for a soul like yours. They love and feel as hard as you do. They have felt pain like you and cherish things just as you do. They may not be a super model but they will awake that love within you. They will be those silent souls that many don't know how to tell them apart but once you speak to them.. you will feel everything within you erupt like a volcano. You'll feel skeptical at first. You'll observe them, study them, analyze them, and little by little you'll feel your soul drifting to them. They'll be that magnetic force that you can't hold back. You'll feel like spilling so much to them but you get scared and worry that they don't feel the same. That's the time you allow your intuition to lead the way. It's the voice of the soul. Connect with them. Tune yourself into them. Feel them as they feel you. You want magic? Allow your soul to do the rest.

Touch her. Kiss her. Love her with all your heart and I'll promise you that you shall have a queen by your side for the rest of your life. She will stand by you when you are feeling weak and understand you in the darkest moments. She will be the one to cherish every single part of your soul. Just love her. Don't hurt her. Be that king she always wanted. Treat her right. Tease her and play with her, but don't fuck with her emotions. If you do, you'll have an enemy for life. Understand her when she is sad and wants time alone. It's not that you did something wrong, it's just she needs that time away from the world to gather all her thoughts and rejuvenate her heart. Help her around the house and do some of the chores. Remember she is not your slave. She is your lady. Support her in all her decisions and if they don't make sense to you, man up and still say I'm here for you and I understand. If she is a little broken.. well my friend, it's not your job to fix her. It's your job to be that soul that will love her no matter what to eternity. The same way she will love you forever.

She ignited fire in all the souls that saw her.

She was beautiful to all. She managed to seduce them with her eyes. A simple stare and they all fell to their knees asking for a hook up. She was gorgeous to me. Not for her physical beauty nor her seductive eyes, but for I saw her past vividly in her daily smiles. She tampered with all my emotions not to hurt me, but just to give me a taste of my own medicine and to show me how much she understood what depth I spoke so much about. Now we're two powerful souls, seeking the unknown knowing that we carry each other's universe within our souls.

Finding you was never my intention.
It was my soul reaching out to yours.

What a marvelous experience when a person allows you to see the beauty they hold within. A feeling that is hard to write.

The outlook they have towards life is remarkable.

When all the outside appearance is peeled away.

When all their flaws are not really flaws.

When the imperfections are perfections.

When their eyes allow you to see the soul but you can see just to an extent.

You are allowed to see the purity they hold. A purity that's so precious and rare but the heart has its own lock. It's a lock that holds so much inside. It holds the pain, betrayal, suffering, and the trust.. but above all things mentioned it holds LOVE.

It holds the love that they desire to giveaway one day, but not just to anyone. They hold that love so tight because they want to give it to the right person. It's hard.

It's hard for the simple reason they don't want to hurt again. They don't want their dreams shattered.

They want to seek and find that perfect person. Not perfection to the way humans understand but perfection from within. Perfection in a way that their life will be complete with the other. That person would be there in good and in bad. That person will be committed to them. Most of all, that person will give them the true love they want. The love that's like flames bursting from within. That just by a glimpse of each other's eyes the future begins to unfold.

As I look deep into your eyes,
I see so much pain and hurt.
I see all the suffering you've had.
The broken promises and abandoned love.
Allow me the opportunity to show you I'm not like the rest.
I don't make promises that I won't keep.
We can build the foundation that we always dreamed.
Together we can be the most powerful relationship that most people seek.
I know what you want, need and desire.
Let's build an empire for our future generations to come.
Allow this intense passion within me to guide you.
In return I'll allow your love to calm my crazy mind.

You were there in my worst times.
You lifted my spirit up on the most troubled days.
Your eyes looked beyond all the outer appearance.
You came and stuck your hand within my body, grabbed
my soul and claimed it as yours.

I will stimulate your mind in such a way
That your soul will feel my presence.
Trust in the direction of your inner guidance.
Believe in this spiritual connection we have.
Allow our minds to elevate into the unknown.
Your soul has found me and I have no intention of letting go.

I have been told that the compatibility between your zo-
diac sign and mine are none.
I have been warned that we can never be in a relationship
that would last.
But to me, no zodiac signs will interfere with the fire that
burns within our souls.

I promise to understand you. I promise to take good care of you. To hold you in my arms and never let go. To grab your heart and hold all the pieces together. When you are feeling weak I will be there to lift your spirit. When you feel like giving up, I will be there to remind you of all the beautiful things you have done. Together we will build a future for generations to come.

Meet me halfway, and watch me cross the line that divides our souls.

It will never matter the distance, time, age or past. When two old souls encounter each other.. The fire within will be felt by both. Their souls will speak to one another in ways that our minds will never understand. Shattered dreams and broken hearts are just stepping stones for these souls when united. Their feelings for each other is best described as internal fireworks. As time passes the fire within will keep bottling up

Although her heart had walls built from titanium, he saw straight through her. He knew it was a challenge but he understood she was worth it, to spend eternity with.

When two individuals are in love, they need to show it to each other daily. It's not just at the beginning.. it's every-day. It's not just a four letter word that you tell a person. You need to show it, express it. It's not just taking in all the good, it's also taking in all the bad too. Compromising is a must. Setting small goals together is one of the keys for longevity. Achieving them united as one is success in a relationship. Many will say live for the moment but in reality you both need to live for the future. When two people have their sights in the future, the moment they are living is the foundation for the generations to come. It's the legacy for them both.

At night when you feel lonely and your thoughts are eating you alive. Just close your eyes and feel my arms around your waist. Listen to my voice whispering in your ear and understand that my soul is here.

We live in a mega-romantic fairy tale, where serendipity stroke our lives daily.

Allow me to scribble art in your heart. For I know when I'm done, your soul will create a poetic masterpiece with it.

In life, we fall in and out of love, but we will always find one person that will cleanse our hearts and get rid of all the past pain. They will open our eyes to something magical. They have this ability to penetrate deep into our souls, and it scares us. It scares us for we never thought this type of person existed in this world. We read about them, hear about them.. but never saw or felt one of them. They come and land their souls on us. They express their passion and love to us that completely leaves us speechless. Most of the time we look at them and ask ourselves, where the fuck have this person been all my life?! Sometimes they come and fall in love with us, and we get scared. We hide thinking why me? We don't believe it. Sometimes, some just come to help us heal from our past. These individuals are ancient warriors that have traveled through many souls in search of their soulmates. They have fought many battles in their lifetime. They know pain and suffering. But one thing is for sure. They have won every time and became warriors of this thing called life. If one of these warriors cross your path, hold on to them. For they will go to any battle for you. For I can assure you, they will win.

Something I have noticed in current relationships is how they show so much affection towards each other in public. You see them and begin to wonder, when will I ever meet someone like that? Or why can't I have that? Just remember, what your eyes see, is not always what is there. We don't know how those couples are in their homes. Sometimes it's all just a show for others. See.. in the outside they can be happy and all cheerful, but in the inside they're probably planning on killing each other. Bottom line is, when you go into a relationship. You make sure there is depth in it. Make sure it's heartfelt and your soul is being stirred. If this is what you are getting, make sure you give it back. The most beautiful thing is a LOVE that's felt within.

And with time, you will be able to understand why the journey took so long. You will see things differently. You will feel things differently. You will no longer look for momentary pleasure. You will begin to seek depth in others. It will not be physical attraction, it will be more soul attraction. It won't be beautiful words they say. It will be the unspoken ones that touch you the most.

I had to burn many bridges, lost plenty friends and gained a lot of enemies. Destroyed myself several times. Just to find the real me after so many tries. And I wouldn't hesitate to do it all over again.

I understand what you feel and I understand what your past has been. Before we knew each other, I already felt your whole life rushing through my veins. Through your eyes, I saw your past but the most beautiful thing that happened was, I felt your soul. Not the way everyone describes it but the way an empath feels it. It was the way I tuned myself to you. Feeling the pain was hard, but feeling your inner purity was priceless. Through my whole life I doubted of the existence of such souls.. but here I am, knowing that the almighty granted me the blessing to feel one such as you walking around this cynical world.

We met in the most beautiful place ever. A place where love is eternal and pain never existed. Where wishes come true and everything was magical.

And when you find that soul that will love you and mean it, it will be something spectacular. Words will never describe it but your soul will shine bright. You will feel something within you that you haven't or never felt. They will come calmly but remember they will have that internal power to destroy all that hurt from your past. It will feel like a magnetic force pulling you towards them. You will try all you can to refuse it, for it's something that you have never felt.. but the fact is, you just can't control yourself. The footsteps this person is leaving on your soul are the trails to the future you envisioned since a young age.

It was that voice that many tried to hear that kept me going. The one that several people tried to study for centuries. That sound that has the power to move mountains and connect with others on a higher level. That depth that so many people give up on. That inner power that several tried to reach but hesitated half way. It's that depth in my soul, I cannot stop until I reach its core. I want to be able to shut off my mind and see everything from a deeper view. I want that power that many speak of. I want to see eyes and feel their life rushing through my body. That power that once the heart stops, my soul will continue roaming and touching souls.

They said don't fall for her. She is not the one for you. They said she is broken, and you can't repair her. They warned me on so many things about her. Me being me, said fuck it. I could fix her. What an egotistical asshole I was. I was the one that never took advice. The worst part was, I didn't allow my intuition to lead the way. My whole point is, we get warned by our friends and family members. They are able to see things from a different view. I was in a stage of wanting a person for her outer appearance. Truth. To my eyes she was a goddess.. I gave everything I had to feel that thing that we call love.. unbelievable. I look back and feel like I bought my way into it. Money can't buy love and what's the use of having a pretty lady by your side when she has a dirty soul? None. Why? They will never have the same life goals as you. They are the ones that live for the moment. That relationship ended on a bad note. I don't regret any of it.. if it wasn't for that bad relationship, I would not be here telling you this or allowing my soul to speak loudly. We both went our separate ways after seven years. I gained something more powerful from it. I gained my intuition back. I had to kill my old self many times to be this person I am today. I would never go back to the old version of me. Now, when I look for love, I seek a deeper connection and understanding. Not just anyone that can stir up my soul. I seek someone that has similar visions for the future. This time.. This time I allow my intuition to lead the path.

Shut the lights and close your eyes. For tonight we will make love in ways unknown to all mankind.

Sometimes in life we fall for different types of people. We fall for them for the way they look, their smiles or the thought of them being the missing link in our lives. We see them as the person we desired so long to accompany us in our journey. Most of the times we fail to see deeper into them. Simply because we fabricate in our minds that they are the ones. We get hurt in our past relationship and look for a supplement to our current situation. It shouldn't be like that. We as humans need that time to heal. Yes, you will heal with time. It's the truth. To some could be months and to others, years. Eventually you will heal. Take the time after your past relationship and take care of yourselves. Be the person you were before the past relationship. Be you. It doesn't matter what people think or say. It's you and that's what matters. Fuck the world and all the people that criticize you. FUCK THEM! Go and do things you never did before within the relationship, and you know what? You will find that person that will fall in love with YOU. I can assure you that. There is a person out there that will love all your flaws and see beauty in you. When you sit in your car or on your bed and wonder how the hell does this person like me? Don't question love.. because when you didn't have someone that liked you, you began to wonder why no one liked you. Bottom line is, be yourself and you will attract a person that will like all of you.

She is a visionary.
Ready to take on the world.
Her soul is one of the purest you will ever find.

Studying me is an obsession.
Analyzing me is an addiction.
Breaking my mind is..
Impossible.

Come on.. let's make magic you and I, together. Let's whisper to each other under the beautiful night while the stars are shining.

Together we will create the most powerful spell.

We have learned to speak to each other without saying a word.

We have mastered the art that no other human have been able to achieve.

You may have imprinted yourself on my heart, but I have been able to touch your mind in so many ways that you didn't even know those parts existed.

Let's stop dancing around in circles and bring yourself towards me.

Together we will release this fire that is burning deep.

When you know the depth of yourself, you become a firm believer in the supreme, magical, powerful and unstoppable force called LOVE.

In a relationship the small gestures mean a lot. Just because others don't do them, doesn't mean you shouldn't. A gentle touch on the cheek or a warm hug can go a long way. You always want to make the other person feel wanted and protected. Cuddling is a simple show of love, but a kiss on the forehead is giving the other assurance that you are there to protect them, in good and bad, take good care of them. Shower them with your love.. deep love. The love that all your previous partners failed to acknowledge.

And when the time is right. You will feel this unexplainable feeling within. Your heart will feel rejuvenated. You will see so many positive things in the other person. They will be in your thoughts throughout the day. You will envision yourself by their presence. Your mind will create a fairytale. Your imagination will make a perfect world for the both of you. Your soul will be starving daily to feel them, you will yearn to touch them, to feel their soft skin against yours, to hear their voice every minute. You will desire to fall asleep and wake up in their arms, you will feel this magical spell over you.. a spell that defines the power of love. You feel it so deep within that it burns the inside of you. You know it's a risk worth taking and definitely worth the wait. When the time is right. You will feel it. You will understand it. Above all, you will cherish it.

How do I know when it's true love? When my heart is able to bleed her love.

In the depth of my words
You will find my soul.

Drift towards the other side. Feel the presence of the un-known. We both know that this fairytale can be turned into reality. Where flesh becomes ashes, souls unite and our passionate love never dies.

And I found you.. through so many eyes that I studied and so many souls I touched, I found you. Millions of whispers I heard daily, but your silent screams seduced me the most.

For many she was a havoc, yet for me she was the shining star that many wished to touch. She wasn't a typical lady like all desired. She was a bad ass that so many feared to get near, but something within her attracted me the most. I yearned to study her inside out. For some reason she was crystalline to my eyes.

Her eyes hold subliminal messages to so many untold stories.

Her heart was a beautiful masterpiece. Not owned by anyone, just created by the magnificent unknown.

In a relationship, the love needs to be demonstrated daily. Not just saying I love you, but showing it. Showing your affection towards each other. You need to understand the language she speaks without speaking it. Understand her goals, desires and needs. Yes, in any relationship there are needs from each other and if you don't know them... ask her. Allow her to share her secrets with you. Don't be the Macho man here. This is not a challenge of who is better than the other. This is a team work, a unity of two souls. Two lovely souls that fell for each other and the goal should be longevity in unity. She trusted you with something that was hard for her to allow anyone in. She gave you her heart. The least you can do is give her your soul in return. She is not perfect and neither are you. And guess what? She knows you are not perfect but she still decided to give you her heart. Now it's time for you to show her your soul.

We spoke below the threshold of sensation. It was the only way we could allow our souls to communicate to each other.

We tasted each other's words before they were written. We lived in each other's thoughts before they were even exposed. We hold on to faith knowing that there is a connection between our souls, and although the desires and the yearnings became deeper as the days went by, we waited for fate to take its place.

I covered the sun with my heart just to see that beautiful glow in your eyes. I aligned all the stars in the sky just to spell out what my soul has been wanting to say to you for so long, and if you still don't understand that I'm just a shy little boy, then a sand castle I shall build.. just so you can feel that within me is your home.

No one will understand the masterpiece she created from the broken pieces. She didn't change for one bit. She just became the lady she always wanted to be. After all the hurt and pain she finally found herself. She found that beauty that was hidden for so long.

No one will never feel her pain. She has fought many battles behind closed doors. Her scars are proof that nothing can stop her.

When you touch her.. Make sure her soul dances to the rhythm of your love.

Two souls believing in the power of love, hesitating in the reality of what they could become. Fearing in what the future could bring but always desiring the fate of the unknown.

Something I learned in this life being single is: Never chase love.. NEVER! Showcase your soul and be honest all the time. Some of us love hard and deep, and some people can't handle it. They never felt that depth we have. Everything will come at the right time. Have faith and believe in that powerful force called LOVE.

I'm not an open book but I am an open soul. Look within and feel the battles I have encountered. See all my fuck ups and understand that I cremated that person. Acknowledge the depth of my soul and study me inside out. Observe every step I take, for soon I will find you. I will touch you in many places you never knew existed. I may bring forth your past, but that's the only way I can make it vanish. I may be an addiction to your thoughts, but is just my way to allure you into my heart. Once you feel my enchantment, you will realize that all along I'm the spirit your soul desired for so long.

It was the breeze she felt inside at the sound of his voice. The calmness and relaxation that her mind needed for so long. Although she knew it was currently just an illusion. Somehow she felt his presence by her side in the darkest moments. She was getting ready. Getting ready to yank his soul from her dreams and bring him to life.

We will never understand the reason why our souls crossed paths.. but with my love, you will never feel deserted, my soul will forever protect you - and my spirit, my spirit will uplift you in all your weakest moments.

It hurts I know.
The pain and suffering.
The restless nights of thinking what you did wrong.
Every night you cry and wonder will you ever be loved again.
Rest assured that you will find that person.
Have faith in LOVE.

Let's allow our past to rest. The lesson has been learned. May our souls lead the way to our destiny and intuition create the path.

I saw you last night for the first time. I stared at your eyes for the longest. Just to get a glimpse of your soul and as I thought. I saw it all. I touched your skin just to feel if what I thought was true and most definitely I was right. Smooth as silk. We spoke for a long time and we both realized that what we felt for each other was on point. We smiled, we joked, we laughed and we just sat there in silence. After seven minutes of no words. You asked me something that penetrated my heart. "Can you please promise me, you will not break my heart?" As a tear crawled down your cheek I gently whispered, I promise you that I will be the protector of your heart. I'll be by your side and within my soul you will forever call your home.

Our souls were preselected to be together before our hearts ever beat.

So many secrets held in her eyes. From the precious moments to the horrific nights. She was known for wearing her heart on her sleeve, when in reality she had her soul scattered in pieces. Shattered were her dreams in this cynical world, until one day she just wrote and released her soul through her powerful words. To inspire and to motivate were her only goals little did she know soon she would be the beautiful unknown.

Two strangers extending their souls sacrificing their hearts desiring the touch of a powerful force called.. love.

We should not allow our hearts to keep playing the guessing game with the soul. Allow the intuition to flow through. Yes. It's a sacrifice. But isn't everything in life a sacrifice?

In love, I go beyond expectations. I will pour my whole soul into a relationship. Death couldn't even stop me. For when death takes place, my soul will still find you.

Sometimes in relationships we expect the other person to read our eyes. We expect them to know exactly what we feel and want to say, but that's not possible. Let's be realistic. If you have something to say, say it. Tell them how you feel. Don't hesitate because you're afraid of their reaction towards it. If it's true love, they will understand. Yes, truth sometimes hurt but it's better than playing the guessing game of what is she/he thinking. We are not Gods. Now when you want to approach your partner and speak of such matters, wait till they are relax and calm.

He wrote every word that came to his mind. He believed in the magic within words. He knew that the only way to her heart was to destroy himself from within.

Sometimes in life we get confused. We confuse our thoughts with intuition. That's one of the hardest things to separate. We fall for people we THINK are the ones. Our minds create this illusion that it feels so real. We begin to constantly fantasize about the future with that person. We see our lives together with them. Our imagination begins to see them as our anchor, and when the loneliness sinks in at night.. oh, how the tears fall down, in hopes that the universe brings them to us. Let's always remember that intuition is not your imagination.

She felt every emotion rising slowly from within. She did everything humanly possible to stop it but the magnetic force was stronger and from a higher level beyond the understanding of the mind.

And although your days feel longer and sometimes no sign of that love you always wanted. Keep in mind and remember that your past mistakes paved the way for that magical love you always desired. That hunger you feel inside of you, the one that keeps your mind running crazy. The feeling that you just want to pour your whole heart to someone. Yes, the one that gives you goosebumps at the thought of it.

And within my darkest moments I found you. I never thought in my life that your soul existed, but you managed to exploit me and bring me back to reality. In your soul I pour my words.. knowing and feeling that you can handle them all. At nights when you lay down and think of all the challenges that life brings, remember that my soul is orbiting in you.

Don't be like the next door person. Be unique. Separate yourself from the others. The way they love, is not the way you love. Be the person that touches souls. Be the person that when you speak you ignite peoples lives in a blink of an eye. Showcase that fire within you.

For a long time she was never herself. She was the person that everyone wanted her to be, but never herself. Lost in time just being someone else. After so much pain and suffering, she finally managed to find her heart. Regaining her inner strength, her past became history and her soul was awakened to the beautiful unknown.

It's such a shame that someone took you for granted. For a beautiful soul like you, I would've given my all just to see a magical future unfold.

I rewired my soul just so it can love you like you always deserved.

We come across some souls in our life, many call them tortured souls. The ones that have encountered pain and suffering from their past. They say that they have so much love to give for they know how it feels to not receive it. They claim those souls have this magical power to heal others. And to be honest, they probably do but let's not call these souls tortured. Let's call them the ancient souls. The healers that many preach about. Yes! The healers of our times.

Tears are just a sign of lessons learned. That's the beautiful language from the soul. When your soul speaks, every part of your body will understand it. For when it's from the soul. Everything surrenders.

Most of the time when we cry, it's not due to pain or hurt. We cry for its the way our soul communicates with us. It's a way for our soul to speak to the heart. Every teardrop is a silent word expressed by the soul. Close your eyes and listen to it. Understand that your soul is being cleansed.

I've seen your eyes and felt your pain. Your heart is settled but your soul is dying to escape. Time flies and still you regret all your mistakes.. breathe.. let it go.. it's over now. Allow your soul to navigate you to the unknown. It's not easy to see things with your eyes closed but it's the only way to understand the unspoken words.

Allow me the opportunity to show you how pure love can be. Shhh, don't cry for I am here now. Close your eyes. Did you feel that? It's pain going away. It's the mending of your heart, the walls collapsing. It's the unknown presence dwelling inside of you. Look into my eyes and understand, Your healing stage has begun.

There is a space available for you in my heart. The last tenant left it all fucked up. Fixing was needed. It's been restored with the best materials unknown to humanity, but there is a catch.. this is not a 1, 2 or 5 year lease. This lease is eternal with no looking back.

In my mind I have traveled to many places in search for comfort. I adapted a different way to look at things. In this transition, my soul is awakened seeking beyond the human eyes.

I just want to gaze into your eyes, jump deep into the ocean of your thoughts. Sink into the bottom of your soul, and I'll make sure to never come up for air.

To truly find love. You will need to forgive your past, it's a must. There is no way around it. When you finally forgive them.. you will be able to heal and love once again.

Your soul will find me.. and when it does, I will make love to it in a way that no one will understand.

Connect with the Author

Website: magesoul.com
Email: magesoul@outlook.com
Instagram: magesoul
Facebook: Magesoul
Twitter: magesoul1

Upcoming poetry books
Precious Pain (July 2018)
Cremating Past (November 2018)

About the Author

Carlos Medina was born and raised in the Bronx, New York. He is known for sharing most of his talent on Instagram and Facebook. His writing began three years ago after a divorce from a five year marriage. Sharing his past pain and healing, he began captivating his readers with his words as he has experienced different facets of life, and has ability to show you the vulnerability of yourself through his words. Traveling through the deepest crevices of your mind, exploring the passages of your heart, you'll be able to explore the depths of your soul and experience memories in ways you never did before.

Made in the USA
Monee, IL
21 October 2021